One Sunday, Seal invited his friends
for supper.

"What's for supper?" said Snail.
"I am serving a sandwich," said Seal.

Seal put some sardines on a slice of bread.
"Sardines in a sandwich!" said Snail.
"That's silly!"

Next Seal added some stew.
"Stew in a sandwich!" said Sloth.
"That's silly!"

Next Seal added some spaghetti.
"Spaghetti in a sandwich!" said Snake.
"That's silly!"

Next Seal added some spinach.
"Spinach in a sandwich!" said Salamander.
"That's silly!"

Next Seal added some scrambled eggs.
"Scrambled eggs in a sandwich!" said Skunk.
"That's silly!"

Next Seal added six scoops
of strawberry ice cream.
"Strawberry ice cream in a sandwich!"
said Spider. "That's silly!"

Next Seal added some salsa and some
maple syrup.
"Salsa and syrup in a sandwich!" said Squirrel.
"That's silly!"

"Who's ready for a slice of my sandwich?"
said Seal.

"No thanks," said Snail, Sloth, Snake, Salamander, Skunk, Spider, and Squirrel. "That sandwich is just too silly!"

But Seal didn't think his sandwich
was silly at all.

He thought it was scrumptious!

How many things can you find that begin with the letter S?

14

See inside back cover for answers.

# Ss Cheer

S is for spider, snake, snail, and seal

S is for a super-sized sandwich meal

S is for sailboat, smile, and sing

S is for spaghetti, seesaw, and swing

Hooray for S, big and small—

the most sensational letter of all!